Scatter Sheets for High-Beginners to Low-Intermediates: ESL Speaking & Vocabulary Lesson Plans for Teenagers & Adults to Improve Fluency

Jackie Bolen

www.eslspeaking.org

Table of Contents

About the Author: Jackie Bolen..5

How to Use this Book...7

Age and Getting Older...8

Animals..10

Appearance..12

Around the Neighborhood...14

Birthdays..16

Business..18

Cars and Driving..20

Childhood...22

Chores..24

Clothes and Fashion...26

Cooking at Home...28

Countries..30

Dating and Marriage..32

Drinking Alcohol...34

Eating Out..36

Exercise..38

Family..40

Food...42

Free Time...44

Getting a Job..46

Habits...50

Holidays...52

Home..54

The Internet..56

Jobs..58

Learning English..60

Movies 62

Pets...64

School Days..66

Travel...70

Before You Go...72

This page intentionally left blank.

About the Author: Jackie Bolen

I taught English in South Korea for a decade to every level and type of student and I've taught every age from kindergarten kids to adults. Most of my time centered around teaching at two universities: five years at a science and engineering school out in the rice paddies of Chungcheongnam-Do, and four years at a major university in Busan where I taught high-level classes for students majoring in English. These days, I live in Vancouver, Canada where I teach privately as well as in English language academies. In my spare time, you can usually find me outside surfing, biking, hiking, or on the hunt for the most delicious kimchi I can find.

In case you were wondering what my academic qualifications are, I hold a Master of Arts in Psychology. During my time in Korea, I completed both the Cambridge CELTA and DELTA certification programs. With the combination of almost 15 years teaching ESL/EFL learners of all ages and levels, and the more formal teaching qualifications I've obtained, I have a solid foundation on which to offer teaching advice. I truly hope that you find this book useful and would love it if you sent me an email with any questions or feedback that you might have—I'll always take the time to personally respond.

Jackie Bolen around the Internet

ESL Speaking (www.eslspeaking.org)

Jackie Bolen (www.jackiebolen.com)

YouTube: https://www.youtube.com/c/JackieBolen

Email: jb.business.online@gmail.com

Also, be sure to check out my other books wherever you like to buy them. Some of the most popular titles include:

101 Activities and Resources for Teaching English Online: Practical Ideas for ESL/EFL Teachers.

39 No-Prep/Low-Prep ESL Speaking Activities: For Teenagers and Adults

39 Awesome 1-1 ESL Activities: For Kids (7-13)

Side Gigs for Teachers: Ways to Actually Make Money

If you can't get enough ESL conversation questions in this book, you can get even more goodness delivered straight to your inbox every week. I promise to respect your privacy —your name and email address will never be shared with anyone for any reason. <u>Sign-up here.</u>

How to Use this Book

These conversation lessons are designed for teenagers, university students or adults. They do assume a very basic knowledge of English grammar and vocabulary so are best suited for high-beginner to low-intermediate students.

The main purpose of these lessons is to get students talking about a certain topic and can be used for classes of 30 minutes to two hours. They are a nice way for English learners to improve their speaking fluency and learn more vocabulary. Each lesson consists of:

- A scatter sheet with related vocabulary words. Have students discuss these words with a partner and look up any words that they don't know. Additionally, discuss some of the more unusual ones as a class.

- A vocabulary challenge with fill-in-the-blank exercises with words from the scatter sheet (along with answers below the discussion questions).

- Discussion questions about each topic.

For smaller classes or 2-4 students, it's possible to work through each lesson together as a class. It's also possible to use these conversation lessons for 1-1 or private tutoring. However, for larger classes of five or more, I recommend putting students into pairs and letting them work through the lesson together to make classes more student-centered.

Age and Getting Older

elementary school

cousins

middle school

infant

children

adults

preschool

high school

seniors

marriage

child

divorce

kindergarten

legal age

nursing home

young

old   getting on in years

middle age

keepsake

mid-life crisis

memories

pregnant

photo album

Vocabulary Challenge

1. My _____ is an _____ which makes it difficult to leave the house.

2. My dad bought a car when he was having a _____.

3. What is the _____ for driving where you live?

4. When I was _____, I played with my _____ a lot.

5. Do you have any _____ from your _____ or _____ days?

Discussion Questions

1. What is the best age to be? Why?

2. What is the most difficult age? Why?

3. Who is the oldest person you know?

4. Is age important to you?

5. Can people of different ages be friends?

6. Are you friends with someone much older or younger?

7. What's a good age to get married?

8. Will you live to be 100?

9. What did you do for your last birthday?

Answers

1. child, infant

2. mid-life crisis

3. legal age

4. young, cousins

5. keepsakes, preschool/kindergarten/elementary school

Animals

Zoo

snake

pork

farm

stripes

extinct

animal rights

spots

giraffe

vegan

animal testing

quit cold turkey

cheetah

pets

wild animals

forest

beef

ocean

fastest

horse

biggest

land animal

lion

shark

whale

zebra

elephant

hamster

Vocabulary Challenge

1. I don't have any _____.

2. A _____ has black and white _____.

3. A _____ is the _____ animal. That's faster than many cars!

4. I think that _____ should not be allowed.

5. _____ is meat that comes from a cow.

Discussion Questions

1. Do you have any pets? In your opinion, what's the best kind of pet?

2. Did you have any pets when you were a kid?

3. Do you have a favorite animal?

4. Are you afraid of any animals?

5. Why are people scared of sharks?

6. Have you seen any movies or read any books with animals in them?

7. What do you think about zoos?

8. Should people be allowed to eat wild animals like snakes, whales, etc.?

Answers

1. pets

2. zebra, stripes

3. cheetah, fastest

4. animal testing

5. beef

Appearance

style

clothes   fashionable

haircut   trendy

beard

pedicure   manicure

shoes

handbag   backpack

scarf

earrings   necklace

nose ring

piercing   sloppy

wedding   formal

well-dressed

facial hair

dressed to kill

tuxedo   black tie event

suit   shades

tie   mustache   hair cut

Vocabulary Challenge

1. A _____ and _____ are examples of _____ on men.

2. Let's get a _____, _____ and _____ before Christmas.

3. What do you think about his _____? I think he might have a difficult time finding a job with it.

4. I need to buy or rent a _____ for the _____ at work.

5. Should I bring my _____ or _____ to work tomorrow? I do need to bring my laptop.

Discussion Questions

1. How often do you get your hair cut?

2. How much money do you spend on a haircut?

3. Have you ever had a pedicure or manicure?

4. What do you think about waxing? Have you ever done it?

5. What kinds of clothes do you like?

6. Do you have a favorite piece of clothing?

7. How much money do you spend on clothes and shoes each month?

8. What do you think about young girls wearing makeup?

9. Do you ever go shopping in sweat pants or pajamas?

Answers

1. beard/mustache, facial hair

2. manicure/pedicure/haircut

3. nose ring

4. tuxedo, black tie event

5. backpack, handbag

Around the Neighborhood

neighbor

restaurant

nightlife

shop

store

parking

fitness center

playground

bus stop

elementary school

middle school

driveway

high school

public transportation

coffee shop

isolated

busy

traffic jam

cafe

fast food restaurant

post office

bank

library

grocery store

community center

trendy

upscale

Vocabulary Challenge

1. When I was young, I could walk to my _____.

2. I exercise at the _____ across the street from me.

3. My street is very _____ and it's difficult to find _____.

4. I like to study at the _____ near me.

5. There's a _____ across the street which makes it easy to get to work.

Discussion Questions

1. What do you like about where you live?

2. What do you not like?

3. Are there any famous things near you?

4. What do you like to do on the weekend?

5. What are some good restaurants near your house?

6. If you want to get a cheap and quick lunch, where do you go?

7. Do you need a car to get around?

8. What are five adjectives to describe your neighborhood (busy, quiet, etc.)?

9. Do you know your neighbors? What are they like?

Answers

1. elementary school

2. community center/fitness center

3. busy, parking

4. coffee shop, cafe, library

5. bus stop

Birthdays

young

old

elderly

senior

teenager

celebrate

party

gift

invite

balloons

streamers

cake

candles

decorations

present

invitations

card

celebration

friends

blow out

game

make a wish

family

surprise party

birthday bash

extended family

dinner

Vocabulary Challenge

1. Don't forget to buy some _____ to put on the _____. We'll need 20 of them!

2. _____ before you _____ the _____ on the _____.

3. My _____ and _____ threw me a _____ for my 50th birthday.

4. Let's make some _____ for your party. Who do you want to _____.

5. Did you buy a _____ for Ted's birthday yet?

Discussion Questions

1. How are birthdays celebrated in your country?

2. Have you ever been to a surprise party? Or organized one?

3. Have you ever forgotten an important birthday?

4. Do you have a memorable past birthday?

5. Are birthdays in your family important? What about at school?

6. What do you think about expensive birthday parties for kids (1-5 years old)?

7. Do you think turning 40 is exciting or sad? (or some other word!)

8. What are some good birthday presents?

9. What did you do for your last birthday?

Answers

1. candles, cake

2. make a wish, blow out, candles, cake

3. family/friends, surprise party

4. invitations, invite

5. gift, present

Business

company   employee

                        employer

boss

        schedule

                vacation   time-off

        weekends   weekday

                    customer service

reviews

        in the red   work from home

                        commute

office   cubicle   desk

        in the black

                    company car   CFO

slogan   website

                            CEO   self-employed

work 'till the death

                corner office   overtime

Vocabulary Challenge

1. Do you have a long _____ to work?

2. Their _____ is terrible. I understand why they have bad _____ online.

3. I can _____ or at the _____. It's my choice.

4. I get lots of _____ time but I do have to work _____.

5. Have you seen the _____ for next week yet? When am I working?

Discussion Questions

1. Are there any companies that you like? Why?

2. Are there any companies that you don't like? Why?

3. Are there any new businesses in your neighborhood?

4. What are some advantages and disadvantages of working for yourself?

5. Would you rather work for someone or work for yourself?

6. Name 5 slogans from companies (Nike—Just do it!).

7. Does every business need a website these days?

8. If you could work in another country, would you choose to do it?

9. Do you like your current job?

Answers

1. commute

2. customer service, reviews

3. work from home, office

4. vacation, weekends

5. schedule

Cars and Driving

commute   SUV

            gas   economy car

minivan   truck

      steering wheel   hybrid

                electric car

                     public transportation

driver's test   license

            learner's permit

      hitch   oil

                     lemon

      gas guzzler

                tires   mechanic

trailer

            oil change   repairs

      warranty   car dealership

station wagon   engine

            manual   automatic

Vocabulary Challenge

1. Let's buy a(n) _____. I don't want to spend so much money on _____.

2. Do you know a good _____? I've been having some problems with my car.

3. If your car is under _____, you won't have to pay for _____.

4. Do you have a _____ on your truck? You need one to pull a _____.

5. My _____ to work is only about 10 minutes.

Discussion Questions

1. What are some advantages and disadvantages to public transportation?

2. How do most people get to work or school in your country?

3. How do you get to work or school?

4. Do you have a driver's license?

5. When did you start driving?

6. Have you ever been in a car accident?

7. Where do you usually drive?

8. Is there a kind of car that you like?

9. Have you ever considered buying an electric car?

Answers

1. electric car/hybrid/economy car, gas

2. mechanic

3. warranty, repairs

4. hitch, trailer

5. commute

Childhood

sister   brother

                          cousins

swimming   siblings

                elementary school

                                    holidays   twin

identical   fraternal

                      summer vacation

        road trip

                                          school trip

                    middle school   high school

teachers   winter vacation

                friends   backyard

        bike ride   playground

                      summer camp   camping

                                                subject

babysitter   TV show

        computer games   video games

Vocabulary Challenge

1. I used to love going _____ during _____.

2. Oh wow! You have a _____. Are you _____ or _____?

3. My favourite _____ in school was English.

4. I have two _____. One _____ and one _____.

5. My favourite thing about _____ was seeing all of my _____.

Discussion Questions

1. What are some memories from childhood?

2. What's your earliest memory?

3. Do you remember any teachers from elementary or school?

4. What was your favorite subject in school?

5. What was your least favorite subject in school?

6. What was your favorite food growing up?

7. Were there foods you didn't like growing up?

8. Did you have a best friend growing up? Do you still talk?

9. Did you play any sports or do any activities during childhood?

Answers

1. swimming, summer vacation

2. twin, identical/fraternal

3. subject

4. siblings, brother/sister

5. holidays, cousins

Chores

wash the dishes

make the bed

do laundry

clean your room

dust

sweep

mop

vacuum

makes dinner

grocery shopping

washer

dryer

laundromat

clean the garage

organize

tidy up

clutter

recycle

Marie Kondo

neat freak

dish rack

take out the trash

pigsty

dirty

messy

washer

dryer

Vocabulary Challenge

1. Tommy! Your bedroom is a _____. Please _____ before you go out.

2. At my house, whoever _____ doesn't have to _____.

3. This weekend, do you want to _____? It has so much _____ that we need to _____.

4. Why don't you _____ and _____ the kitchen floor and I'll _____ the bedrooms?

5. My new place doesn't have a _____ and _____ so I have to go to the _____.

Discussion Questions

1. What chores do you spend a lot of time doing?

2. What are some chores that you don't mind?

3. What are some chores that you hate?

4. Is there a way to make chores fun?

5. Do you have kids? If yes, what chores do they do?

6. Do you prefer doing laundry every couple of days or once a week?

7. Do you wash your dishes after every meal?

8. How often do you vacuum?

9. Who does most of the chores at your house?

Answers

1. pigsty, tidy up

2. makes dinner, wash the dishes

3. clean the garage, clutter, organize

4. sweep, mop, vacuum

5. washer, dryer, laundromat

Clothes and Fashion

Black Friday   pants

                         stores   leggings

              style   shoes

socks   shirt

              sweater   hoodie

                    trend   expensive

brand name

                                   thrift store

                    donate   window shopping

         accessories   jewelry

closet   dresser   drawer

sandals   casual

              formal   suit

       jeans   tie

              dress   skirt   blouse

                    scarf   sweater

online shopping   handbag

Vocabulary Challenge

1. I prefer _____ to going to _____.

2. _____ clothes like Gucci and Prada are too _____ for me.

3. My clothes barely fit into my _____ and _____.

4. I don't like _____ and _____ and prefer to wear _____ on my feet, even in winter.

5. You can't wear _____ and a _____ to a job interview!

Discussion Questions

1. Are clothes important to you?

2. Do you like shopping at thrift stores? Why or why not?

3. Do you like shopping?

4. How often do you go clothes shopping?

5. What are some of the advantages of shopping online?

6. What are some of the disadvantages of shopping online?

7. What's the most you've ever spent on a single article of clothing?

8. Do you follow clothing trends?

9. What are some strange fashion trends that you've seen?

Answers

1. online shopping, stores

2. brand name, expensive

3. closet/dresser

4. socks/shoes, sandals

5. jeans, hoodie

Cooking at Home

breakfast   gluten-free

knife   cutting board   lunch

dinner   snack

brunch   make dinner

wash the dishes   can opener

whole foods   dishwasher

fork   picky eater   knife

food processor   dishes

spoon

cutlery   plate   bowl

eating out   take out meal

stove   oven

microwave   frozen meals

instant food   frying pan

processed food   vegan

vegetarian   diet

healthy   unhealthy

Vocabulary Challenge

1. I'm so _____ and eat too much _____.

2. I'm a _____ but my son is a _____ so I always have to make two meals!

3. Here's a _____ and _____. Please chop up these vegetables for the salad.

4. Where's your _____ drawer? I need a _____ for my soup.

5. Please put your _____ in the _____ after every meal.

Discussion Questions

1. In one week, how often do you eat out?

2. In one week, how often do you get take-out?

3. Are you a good cook?

4. What are some of the meals you regularly cook?

5. Do you like cooking with meat? Are you a vegan (no animal products)?

6. Do you eat anything special for weekend breakfasts?

7. How often do you eat with other people?

8. Do you enjoy cooking a big holiday or family meal?

9. What's the first thing you learned how to cook?

Answers

1. unhealthy, instant food/processed food

2. vegan/vegetarian, picky eater

3. cutting board, knife

4. cutlery, spoon

5. dishes, dishwasher

Countries

North America   natural resources

           economy   Europe

     biggest   Central America

           South America   flight

                         Africa

Pacific Ocean   Atlantic Ocean

           visa   crowded

                smallest   population

     economy   tourism

                allies   world tour   EU

international travel   all-inclusive resort

                         languages

           pride   political system

sleepy   global

           president   prime minister

     passport   tourist destination

Vocabulary Challenge

1. Canada has a _____ but the USA has a _____.

2. Canada has two official _____, English and French.

3. You need a _____ if you want to go to another country. Some places also require a _____.

4. The _____ country is Russia.

5. Canada has many _____ like oil and gas.

Discussion Questions

1. How would you describe your country?

2. What are the most famous places in your country?

3. What are the major holidays in your country?

4. Are there any famous foods that your country is known for?

5. Have you ever visited another country?

6. Is there a country you want to visit?

7. If you could take a world tour for 6 months, where would you visit?

8. What is the perfect length of time for a vacation?

9. What's one of the best countries? Why?

Answers

1. prime minister, president

2. languages

3. passport, visa

4. biggest

5. natural resources

Dating and Marriage

date

red flags

tuxedo

husband

wife

fiance

first date

boyfriend

girlfriend

online dating

kiss

gay marriage

arranged marriage

romantic

blind date

wedding

cake

engaged

party

bridesmaids

best man

ring

wedding dress

honeymoon

divorce

sole custody

shared custody

partner

divorce rate

Vocabulary Challenge

1. Did you notice any _____ on your _____ with that new guy?

2. I heard that you got _____. Can I see your _____?

3. How many _____ are you having at your _____?

4. I want to go to Italy for my _____.

5. My ex-_____ and I have _____ of our children.

Discussion Question

1. Have you tried online dating? How did it go?

2. Is dating common among your friends?

3. At what age do people usually get married?

4. Do you have any interesting or funny dating experiences?

5. If you have a partner, how did you meet?

6. Do you want to get married?

7. What are the positives of marriage?

8. What are the negative things about marriage?

9. What do you think about arranged marriages?

Answers

1. red flags, first date

2. engaged, ring

3. bridesmaids, wedding

4. honeymoon

5. husband/wife, shared custody

Drinking Alcohol

beer
wine

hard liquor

glass
pint
shots

shot glass

mixed drink
pub
bar

open bar

party

go for drinks
drunk

tipsy

drinking and driving

drunk driving

hangover
designated driver (DD)

legal drinking age

alcohol
ID

home brewing
wasted

underage
fake ID

Vocabulary Challenge

1. Is there an _____ at your wedding?

2. Can I please get a _____ of _____? The lager, please.

3. Drink some water or you'll have a _____ tomorrow.

4. I'll be the _____. I don't want anyone _____.

5. Let's have some _____. Do you like whisky?

Discussion Questions

1. What is the drinking age in your country?

2. Is the drinking age too young, too old, or just right?

3. Is there social pressure for people to drink alcohol where you live?

4. What do you think about driving a car after drinking?

5. In your opinion, how many drinks can someone have and still drive?

6. If you drink, do you like beer, wine, or something else?

7. Who do you usually drink with?

8. When do you usually drink alcohol?

9. Have you ever had a hangover?

Answers

1. open bar

2. pint/glass, beer

3. hangover

4. designated driver, drinking and driving

5. shots

Eating Out

restaurant   cafe

                              coffee shop

to go   take-out   dine in

                              menu   chef

        tip   drink

appetizer   go dutch   main course

                    dessert

                              chain restaurant

kid's menu   server

                    waiter   waitress

        bartender   dishwasher

                    gluten-free

busboy/busgirl

                    cook   tax

        check   split the check

                    reservation

patio   non-smoking

Vocabulary Challenge

1. It's usually busy on Friday night. Should we make a _____?

2. Can I get you something to _____?

3. I'm not sure if it's _____. I'll check with the _____.

4. I worked as a _____ in high school. It was so tiring and hot.

5. Should we get _____ or _____?

Discussion Questions

1. How often do you eat out?

2. What meal do you eat out for most often? (breakfast, lunch or dinner)

3. What's your favorite restaurant?

4. Where do you go for a cheap, quick meal?

5. What do you think about fast-food restaurants?

6. Do you prefer chain restaurants or independent ones?

7. Do you think restaurants are cheap, too expensive or just right?

8. Is tipping at restaurants common? What's a good percentage to tip?

9. Do you ever get take-out?

Answers

1. reservation

2. drink

3. gluten-free, chef/cook

4. dishwasher

5. take-out, dine in

Exercise

healthy   unhealthy

            cardio   lifting weights

    gym   fitness center

                yoga   sports

team sports   cycling

            running   racket sports

    athlete   weekend warrior

                gym class

        hiking   injured

gym class

                high blood pressure   heart attack

                                                out of shape

            in shape   indoors

outdoors   membership

                swimming   class

    doctor   trainer

fitness class   orientation

Vocabulary Challenge

1. I'm a _____ and only play _____ every few months.

2. My doctor said that I had a _____ because I'm so _____.

3. Did you like _____ when you were in school?

4. I enjoy _____ like badminton or tennis.

5. I like to exercise _____ more than _____.

Discussion Questions

1. How often do you exercise?

2. Do you like sports like running, swimming or cycling?

3. Name 5 team sports.

4. Name 5 individual sports.

5. Do you prefer to exercise indoors or outdoors?

6. Do you have a favourite sports team?

7. Do you think you're healthy?

8. How often should kids have gym (physical education) classes in school?

9. Did you learn to swim when you were a kid?

Answers

1. weekend warrior, sports

2. heart attack, out of shape/unhealthy

3. gym class

4. racket sports

5. indoors/outdoors

Family

niece   nephew

aunt   uncle

                                        grandparents

        sister   brother   divorced

cousins   stepmother

            remarried   stepfather

        siblings   family

                    growing up

fight   bedroom

                holidays   children

married

                        wedding

    extended family   twins   only child

                    grandfather

        chores   after school

                    vacation

grandmother   second cousin

40

Vocabulary Challenge

1. I have a very large _____.

2. My parents got _____ when I was little and only my mom got _____.

3. I did lots of _____ when I was young. For example, cleaning my room and washing the dishes.

4. My sister is _____ but I don't have a _____ or _____.

5. I only know two _____ and they are my _____.

Discussion Questions

1. Who are the people in your family that are important to you?

2. Is family important to you?

3. Do you have any really good friends who are like family?

4. What are some of the advantages of being an only child?

5. What are some of the advantages of having many brothers or sisters?

6. Did you have any chores growing up?

7. Did you have to keep your room clean when you were a child?

8. Did you use to spend a lot of time with your grandparents?

9. Do you have lots of cousins? Did you spend time with them when you were young?

Answers

1. extended family

2. divorced, remarried

3. chores

4. married, niece/nephew

5. twins, cousins

Food

healthy   unhealthy

fruits and vegetables   meat

grain   beans

sugar   fat

salt   home cooking

eating out   meal prep box

take-out   junk food

candy   deep fried

wheat   rice

restaurant   corn

vegan   gluten-free

tofu   vegetarian

couch potato

dairy   a piece of cake

pickled   breakfast

lunch   dinner

snack   brunch

Vocabulary Challenge

1. I'm a _____ so I eat a lot of _____ and _____.

2. I can't drink milk. I get a sore stomach when I have _____.

3. Don't worry about it. That test is _____.

4. Does that _____ have any _____ things to eat? I get really sick if I eat _____.

5. Let's have an early _____. I skipped breakfast.

Discussion Questions

1. What are some foods that you don't like?

2. Name 10 healthy foods.

3. Name 10 unhealthy foods.

4. What do you usually eat for breakfast?

5. What do you usually eat for lunch?

6. What do you usually eat for dinner?

7. Does your family eat dinner together?

8. What's your favorite kind of food? (Italian, Chinese, Korean, etc.)

9. What's your favorite restaurant?

Answers

1. vegan/vegetarian, beans/tofu

2. dairy

3. a piece of cake

4. restaurant, gluten-free, wheat

5. lunch

Free Time

weekdays   weekend

                    binge watch   sleeping in

hanging out   exercise

                                                        overtime

            watch a flick

    cleaning   playing sports

                    chilling out

spending time with friends

                                        catch some rays

            shoot some hoops

        streaming   download   Candy Crush

            stress   busy

road trip   getaway

                                        4-day work week

            work phone   splurge

    all-nighter

            have some drinks   relax

Vocabulary Challenge

1. Are you busy this _____? Let's take a _____ to Whistler.

2. My son loves _____ and doesn't get up until 2:00 in the afternoon.

3. My trip to Salt Spring Island was a nice _____. I feel very refreshed.

4. My weekend was terrible. I worked _____ and did some _____ in my garage.

5. Enjoy your trip and don't take your _____ with you!

Discussion Questions

1. Do you like to watch movies or TV in your free time?

2. Do you exercise in your free time?

3. How much free time do you usually have on weekdays?

4. Do you wish that you had more free time?

5. Do you ever have to work late?

6. How much free time do you have on weekends?

7. Do you like to sleep in late?

8. Do you like to stay at home or go out?

9. What are some things to do on weekends in your city?

Answers

1. weekend, road trip

2. sleeping in

3. getaway

4. overtime, cleaning

5. work phone

Getting a Job

job application

resume

CV   cover letter

interview

suit and tie   dress shoes

applicants

screening   skills test

full-time job

benefits

part-time job   education

experience

job market

vacation time   flex days

unlimited vacation   apply online

internship

language skills   follow-up interview

salary   upgrading

Vocabulary Challenge

1. The _____ is low but there's lots of _____.

2. I already have a _____ but I need to buy some _____ for my interview.

3. I don't have much _____ but I do have great _____. I speak French, German and English.

4. Do you know how many _____ there are for this job?

5. You can _____ for that job. You don't even need a _____ or _____.

Discussion Questions

1. What's a good job that you've had?

2. What's a bad job that you've had?

3. Did you have any part-time jobs in school?

4. How did you get your current job?

5. What is the most common way to get a job in your country?

6. What do you think about photos on job applications?

7. Is it easy or difficult to get a job in your country?

8. Do you have any tips on how to dress for a job interview?

9. What information do you have to include on a resume?

Answers

1. salary, vacation time

2. suit and tie, dress shoes

3. experience, language skills

4. applicants

5. apply online, resume, cover letter

Going to a Party

invitation   dressing up

           gift   present

invite

                    party favour

           food   snacks

     birthday   anniversary

                                   wedding

           holiday

RSVP   music   playlist

                    potluck

     buffet   appetizer

     drinks   host

hostess   mask

                Halloween

     dance party   theme-party

           costume   makeup

surprise party   venue

Vocabulary Challenge

1. Are you wearing a _____ to Ted's _____ party?

2. How many people are you going to _____?

3. Did you _____ to Jen and Carrie's _____ _____ yet?

4. I'm planning on bringing spaghetti with tomato sauce to the _____.

5. What about _____? Can you make a _____?

Discussion Questions

1. What was the last party you went to?

2. Did your school or workplace have any parties this year?

3. Do you prefer big or small parties?

4. Do you bring a gift to the host of the party?

5. Have you ever been to a surprise party?

6. Would you be happy if someone threw you a surprise party?

7. How much do you regularly spend on birthday gifts?

8. Have you ever been to a potluck party?

9. Is it impolite to click attending on Facebook for a party but not go?

Answers

1. costume, Halloween

2. invite

3. RSVP, wedding, invitation

4. potluck

5. music, playlist

Habits

healthy

unhealthy

sleeping in

a morning person

a night owl

stay up late   junk food

fruits and vegetables

exercise

smoking

drinking

quit cold turkey   quit smoking

New Year's Resolution

bad habits

good habits

fidgeting

chewing gum

sin tax

enough sleep

fast food

Vocabulary Challenge

1. Are you _____ or _____?

2. I never _____ because I _____.

3. I love to go out _____ with my friends at the pub.

4. Tim! Do you ever sit still? Stop _____.

5. My _____ is to eat more _____.

Discussion Questions

1. Name five healthy habits.

2. What are some of your healthy habits?

3. Name five unhealthy habits.

4. What are some of your unhealthy habits?

5. Do you ever sleep in?

6. How often do you exercise?

7. Are you annoyed by someone chewing gum loudly?

8. Do you think people should be allowed to smoke inside?

9. Should people be allowed to drink alcohol in public?

Answers

1. a night owl/a morning person *or* healthy/unhealthy

2. get enough sleep, stay up late

3. drinking

4. fidgeting

5. New Year's resolution, fruits and vegetables

Holidays

Christmas   Easter

                            St. Patrick's Day

ham   Valentine's Day

                            Thanksgiving

            Black Friday

                        New Year's Eve   Christmas Eve

Christmas Day   Boxing Day

                            Buy Nothing Day

            Labour Day   celebrate

                                    turkey

                    Cupid   stuffing

American football   present

            mashed potatoes   Santa Claus

                            North Pole

        reindeer   Christmas carols

                    pilgrims   card

            stocking

Vocabulary Challenge

1. _____ is in February and celebrates love.

2. _____ is the day that you should wear green.

3. _____ is on December 25th.

4. _____, _____, _____, and _____ are some popular holiday foods.

5. You can find some good deals on _____.

Discussion Questions

1. What are some special holiday foods?

2. Is gift-giving a part of the holidays?

3. Do people decorate their houses during the holidays?

4. What's your favorite holiday? Why?

5. What was your favorite holiday when you were a kid?

6. Do you spend most holidays like Christmas with your family?

7. Have you ever done anything unusual for a holiday?

8. What are some favourite holiday memories?

9. Have you ever had a big holiday dinner or party before?

Answers

1. Valentine's Day

2. St. Patrick's Day

3. Christmas/Christmas Day

4. turkey, stuffing, ham, mashed potatoes

5. Boxing Day/Black Friday

Home

roommates

den

living room

bedroom

kitchen

garage

front yard

backyard

reno

apartment

rent

mortgage

washer

dryer

stairs

basement suite

dishwasher

oven

stove

storage shed

dresser

patio

bathroom

landlord

tenant

cozy

homey

relaxing

basement

plants

Vocabulary Challenge

1. I keep my bicycle in a _____ in the _____.

2. I hate washing dishes and I'll never live in a place without a _____.

3. I live in a _____. It's okay but it's quite cold in winter.

4. I don't have a _____ or _____ at my house so I have to use the laundromat.

5. My apartment is small, only a _____, _____, _____ and _____.

Discussion Questions

1. Describe the home or apartment you live in.

2. Describe your neighborhood.

3. Do you know any of your neighbors? What are they like?

4. Do you live alone or with other people?

5. What are some of your favorite things to do at home?

6. Do you like to meet friends out or at your house?

7. Do you have any pets?

8. Do you have a backyard? What are some advantages and disadvantages of this?

9. Do you need a car where you live?

Answers

1. storage shed, backyard

2. dishwasher

3. basement suite

4. washer/dryer

5. bedroom/bathroom/living room/kitchen

The Internet

speed

Internet service provider (ISP)

IP address   modem

addicted   high-speed Internet

dial-up   device

smartphone

laptop   online   offline

in real life   online dating   URL

work from home

gaming computer   direct message

(DM)

private message (PM)

streaming   password

username   security

gaming   battery

charger   fast

slow   loading   website

Vocabulary Challenge

1. Where is my _____? My _____ is running low.

2. My friend is _____ to _____. He does it all night with his friends and doesn't sleep much.

3. This _____ isn't _____. I just want to buy the movie tickets!

4. Do you have some _____ friends that you've never met _____?

5. Never tell anyone your _____ and _____ for online banking!

Discussion Questions

1. Name 5 negative things about the Internet.

2. How do you spend most of your time on the Internet?

3. How many hours a day are you online?

4. How do you usually access the Internet? (kind of device)

5. Do you need to use the Internet for school or work?

6. Are you addicted to your smartphone?

7. What are the negatives of spending too much time online?

8. How nervous do you feel if your phone is running low on battery?

9. Should parents limit how much time children spend on electronics?

Answers

1. charger, battery

2. addicted, gaming

3. website, loading

4. online, in real life

5. username, password

Jobs

university   white-collar

          blue-collar   college

degree   experience

       references   education

   resume   cover letter

boss   day shift

         night shift   factory

      manual labour   service

industry

     9-5   overtime   statutory holiday

      employee

             coworkers

vacation   benefits   dental

        pension

   pay   retire

    quit   job search

apply online   screening

Vocabulary Challenge

1. I _____ my job because I hated working the _____.

2. The _____ isn't that high but there is 6 weeks of _____ and excellent _____.

3. I'm getting too old to work in _____ jobs.

4. My _____ are so fun! It makes my job so good.

5. Please send me your _____ and _____. I'll give them to my _____.

Discussion Questions

1. Name 10 jobs for which you need a university degree.

2. Name 10 jobs for which you don't need a university degree.

3. Name 10 jobs where people have to work at night or on the weekend.

4. What did you want to be growing up?

5. Describe your job now (or plan for after graduation).

6. What's a typical day at your job like?

7. How often do you work overtime?

8. Do you ever work on weekends or holidays?

9. What's a very good job in your country?

Answers

1. quit, night shift

2. pay, vacation, benefits

3. blue-collar, manual labour

4. coworkers

5. resume/cover letter, boss

Learning English

grammar   vocabulary

      exam   motivation

  speaking   required

               writing   reading

      listening   boring

interesting

      optional   flashcards

        app   mandatory

class   study partner

  teacher   student

       first language

    native speaker   second language

ESL   EFL

             no pain, no gain

cutting corners   study

    course   study tip   IELTS

Vocabulary Challenge

1. This English _____ is _____.

2. What's your _____ for studying English?

3. My _____ is Korean and my _____ is English.

4. I use _____ on the bus or subway to learn _____.

5. You have to study to improve your English! _____.

Discussion Questions

1. Why are you studying English?

2. Is studying English mandatory in schools in your country?

3. What do you find easy about learning English?

4. What do you find difficult about learning English?

5. Are you studying any other languages?

6. Do you prefer studying alone, with a partner, or with a teacher?

7. Do you prefer speaking/listening or reading/writing?

8. Do you enjoy watching English TV shows or movies?

9. Have you ever done an English test like the IELTS, TOEFL or TOEIC

Answers

1. class/course, optional/mandatory/boring/interesting

2. motivation

3. first language, second language

4. flashcards, vocabulary

5. no pain, no gain

Movies

actor   actress

movie star   director

sound   special effects

location   studio

animation   action   drama

comedy

private life   funny

boring   interesting

producer

paparazzi   surprising

filming

gossip   Hollywood

Academy awards   streaming

movie theater

home theater   expensive

popcorn   celebrity

junk food   snacks

Vocabulary Challenge

1. I love _____ like Mission Impossible with lots of _____.

2. Which _____ was this movie filmed in? Was it Vancouver?

3. My favourite thing about going to the _____ is getting some _____ to eat.

4. Who is the main _____? He's so good!

5. Do you keep up to date with _____ _____?

Discussion Questions

1. What was the last movie you saw?

2. What's a movie you've watched many times?

3. Do you have any favorite actors or actresses?

4. Do you prefer watching movies in your first language or English?

5. Where do you like to watch movies?

6. Do you think movie theaters are too expensive?

7. How often do you watch a movie?

8. Are there any snacks you like to eat while watching a movie?

9. Do you have a favourite movie?

Answers

1. action movies, special effects,

2. location

3. movie theater, popcorn

4. actor

5. celebrity, gossip

63

Pets

dogs

cats

hamster

fish

rat

sloth

snakes

lizard

dog park

cage

litter box

tank

collar

toys

treat

pet store

pet food

responsibility

adopt

breeder

seeing eye dog

advantage

disadvantage

energetic

reptile

turtle

exotic

fur

extinct

shedding

feeding

man's best friend

animal testing

Vocabulary Challenge

1. _____ and _____ are the most common pets around the world.

2. Some blind people have a _____.

3. Pets can help teach kids about _____.

4. I give my dog a _____ whenever she does a trick.

5. Many people are scared of _____.

Discussion Questions

1. Do you have any pets?

2. Did you have any pets growing up? Did you get them for a Christmas present?

3. Do you ever watch cute or funny animal videos?

4. If you could have a pet in the future, what kind would you like?

5. What are some advantages of pets?

6. What are some disadvantages of pets?

7. Have you ever seen a "seeing eye dog" for a blind person before?

8. Are you afraid of any animals?

9. Are pets good for children?

Answers

1. dogs/cats

2. seeing eye dog

3. responsibility

4. treat

5. snakes

School Days

pep rally

elementary school

physics

high school

recess

English

memories

middle school

after school

lunchtime

chemistry

math

cafeteria

club

sports teams

biology

teacher

principal

assistant principals

volunteer

community service

P.E.

detention

suspension

uniform

locker

band

science

French

subject

winter vacation

spring break

Spanish

summer vacation

history

Vocabulary Challenge

1. My favourite _____ was _____. I loved playing all kinds of sports.

2. My _____ was very big and had 1 _____ and 4 _____.

3. At _____, I used to play basketball with my friends.

4. The food at the _____ in high school was terrible!

5. My family used to go camping during _____.

Discussion Questions

1. What's a favorite memory from elementary school?

2. What's a favorite memory from middle or high school?

3. What sports did you play or clubs did you join in school?

4. Who was your favourite teacher?

5. What was your favorite subject?

6. What was your least favourite subject?

7. What are some qualities of a good teacher?

8. What are some qualities of a bad teacher?

9. What's the purpose of school and education?

Answers

1. subject, P.E.

2. high school, principal, assistant principals

3. lunchtime

4. cafeteria

5. summer vacation

Time

weekend   weekday

morning person

night owl

free time   month

year   week

bi-weekly   afternoon

morning   evening

time is money

school night

alarm   Monday

Tuesday   Thursday

Wednesday

Friday   Sunday

Saturday   after

before   until

decade   leisure time   calendar

Vocabulary Challenge

1. Thursday is the day before _____ and the day after _____.

2. I'm not a _____ but I have to start work at 6:30 in the morning. It's terrible.

3. Let's get back to work. _____!

4. It's time for bed. Remember that it's a _____.

5. Should I set the _____ for 7:30?

Discussion Questions

1. What do you like to do in your free time?

2. Do you think you have enough free time?

3. What would you do if you had an extra three hours each day?

4. What does your work or study time look like?

5. What's your busiest day of the week?

6. What's your most relaxing day?

7. What time do you usually get up?

8. What time do you go to bed at night?

9. Are you ever late for things? What usually causes this?

Answers

1. Friday, Wednesday

2. morning person

3. time is money

4. school night

5. alarm

Travel

airplane

train   visa   seat sale

flight

window   aisle

road trip

backpacking   car

bus   cycling

resort

tourist destination   reviews

attractions

dream vacation   passport

study abroad

school trip   taxi

Uber   AirBnB

non-smoking

ferry   all-inclusive

Vocabulary Challenge

1. Should we take an _____, _____ or _____ to the concert?

2. My _____ would be to go _____ around South-East Asia.

3. To get to Salt Spring Island, you have to take a _____.

4. My favourite _____ was when my class went to Ottawa.

5. There's a big _____ until Friday. Let's book something!

Discussion Questions

1. Have you ever taken a trip outside your country?

2. What's a memorable vacation you've taken?

3. Do you have any future travel plans coming up?

4. What would your dream vacation look like?

5. Did you go on an interesting school trip when you were a kid?

6. When you travel, do you like to stay close to home or go to other countries?

7. Do you prefer summer or winter vacations?

8. Have you ever had your passport, phone, or wallet stolen when travelling?

9. Could you live in another country for the rest of your life?

Answers

1. Uber/taxi/bus

2. dream vacation, backpacking/cycling

3. ferry

4. school trip

5. seat sale

Before You Go

Thanks for using this book of conversation lessons. I hope that you've found it useful. If you liked the book, please consider leaving a review wherever you bought it. It'll help other teachers, like yourself, find this useful resource.

Also, be sure to check out my other books wherever you like to buy them. Some of the most popular titles include:

101 Activities and Resources for Teaching English Online: Practical Ideas for ESL/EFL Teachers.

39 No-Prep/Low-Prep ESL Speaking Activities: For Teenagers and Adults

39 Awesome 1-1 ESL Activities: For Kids (7-13)

Side Gigs for Teachers: Ways to Actually Make Money

If you can't get enough conversation lessons in this book, you can get even more goodness delivered straight to your inbox every week. I promise to respect your privacy—your name and email address will never be shared with anyone for any reason. Sign-up here.

Made in the USA
Middletown, DE
20 September 2023

38866100R00042